The Dragon, the Prince, and the Flemglobber
An Olde Hanukkah Tale

Copyright © 2025 Irv Korman

All rights reserved. No part of this book may be used or reproduced in any manner whatsoever without written permission of the publisher, except in the case of brief quotations embodied in critical articles and reviews. For permission requests, write to publisher, at email address below.

ISBN 978-1-948613-27-9
Library of Congress Control Number: 2025910527

Printed in the United States of America

Sunny Day Publishing, LLC
Cuyahoga Falls, Ohio 44223
www.sunnydaypublishing.com
editor@sunnydaypublishing.com

For "Brother Liam"

Acknowledgements

This book would not have been possible without the help and encouragement of:

Kristen Ely
Francine Korman
Julie Korman
Melanie Korman
Elsbeth O'Connor
Barbara Renstrom

A very special "thank you" to Bill O'Connor for taking the time to read the manuscript and the giving of his valuable time, continued help, advice and suggestions to this author, especially on the monastic life.

The Dragon, The Prince, and The Flemglobber

An Olde Hanukkah Tale

Irv Korman

An Olde Hanukkah Tale

Once upon a time, in the realm of Fargessen, nestled along the shores of the enchanting Fanta Sea, our tale unfolds. This kingdom, long lost in the annals of history, found its place between the neighboring realms of Vulgaria and Dorton.

Stretching from its northern borders was a slender strip of land, reaching out into the depths of the Fanta Sea—a peninsula adorned with the wonders of nature. And at the very tip of this peninsula stood the pride of Fargessen: Mount Batten, a beacon of majesty and grandeur.

The Dragon, The Prince, and The Flemglobber

At the peak of Mount Batten, overlooking Hamilton Beach, stood the renowned monastery of St. Bernard of Dogma, under the guidance of Abbot Costello. Revered across distant lands, this sanctuary owed its fame to the remarkable healing properties of the steam rising from two adjacent mountain springs: one hot, the other cold. Discovered by Brother Bach, a Benedictine monk of the monastery, the merging vapors proved to be a panacea for ailments of all kinds. The convergence point of these streams was christened "Bach's Spring" in honor of the monk's revelation. Abbot Costello and his brethren dedicated themselves to ensuring the comfort of travelers who sought respite at St. Bernard of Dogma, offering them solace amidst the curative mists of Bach's Spring.

Below the summit of Mount Batten reigned the once-forgotten Kingdom of Fargessen, under the rule of King Dominic, affectionately known as King Dom, alongside his wife, Queen Sighs, and their son, Prince Hipple.

While King Dom attended to the affairs of the realm, Queen Sighs devoted herself to composing cheerful, whimsical tunes, strumming her two 15-string lutes with the

An Olde Hanukkah Tale

accompaniment of her nieces, Rosette Pickguard and Peg Fretboard.

Meanwhile, Prince Hipple, the kingdom's future sovereign, shadowed his father diligently, absorbing wisdom and garnering popularity among the people.

The bustling heart of Fargessen was Tolemac, its capital city. Tolemac held unparalleled significance due to its pivotal role as the nexus of trade. All goods produced within the kingdom departed via Tolemac's main road, while external commodities entered through the same thoroughfare. Thus, the perpetual clearance of Tolemac's main road was paramount, ensuring seamless commerce within and beyond the realm.

One fateful day, chaos struck the Kingdom of Fargessen as Tolemac's main road came to an abrupt halt, paralyzed by an immense and immovable obstruction. The culprit? None other than Finnog!

The Dragon, The Prince, and The Flemglobber

Finnog, the legendary fire-breathing dragon, had settled himself squarely in the middle of the main road just before the impending holiday of Hanukkah, refusing to budge an inch.

In a flurry of urgency, King Dom summoned Queen Sighs, Prince Hipple, and his trusted advisors to Kenahora Castle to devise a plan for Finnog's removal. With Hanukkah looming and Prince Hipple's fervent anticipation of the holiday, swift action was imperative.

Despite relentless efforts—including hurling stones, dousing Finnog with scalding water and boiling oil, and launching the kingdom's sharpest projectiles—Finnog remained obstinate, unmoved by any measure taken against him.

With tensions rising, King Dom resorted to a desperate measure: he called upon the music students of Tolemac Conservatory of Music. Their task? To serenade Finnog with off-key tunes, played on untuned instruments, in hopes of coaxing him away from the road. Yet, even this unconventional attempt failed to rouse the dragon.

Finnog's steadfast refusal to budge stemmed

from a simple reason: lieberries. These succulent fruits, Finnog's favorite delicacy, flourished on bushes flanking Tolemac's main road. Positioned at the heart of the lieberry patch, which conveniently coincided with the road, Finnog indulged in his feast without needing to relocate.

As Hanukkah drew near, Tolemac remained paralyzed, with Finnog showing no signs of budging. King Dom's spirits sank, mirrored by Queen Sighs, whose songs turned mournful, and even her nieces, Rosette Pickguard and Peg Fretboard, ceased their melodies.

The Dragon, The Prince, and The Flemglobber

Realizing Hanukkah's festivities were threatened by Finnog's blockade, King Dom summoned Prince Hipple urgently to Kenahora Castle.

"Son," began King Dom, "I have a crucial task for you."

Curious, Prince Hipple inquired, "What is it, father?"

"You must venture into Fargessen Forest," declared the king.

An Olde Hanukkah Tale

Alarmed, Prince Hipple voiced his concerns about the forest's reputation for darkness and danger, but King Dom assured him of its significance in solving royal dilemmas.

Though apprehensive, Prince Hipple resolved to heed his father's plea, spurred by his loyalty to the kingdom and his love for Hanukkah.

After receiving his father's directions, Prince Hipple embarked on his journey to Fargessen Forest at dawn, determined to fulfill his mission.

After hours of travel, Prince Hipple arrived at the forest and found a clearing with a prominent tree stump. Exhausted, he sat down, resting his head on the stump, reminiscing about Hanukkah and his family's traditions.

As he drifted into thoughts of festivities and Finnog's blockade, he felt a tap on his shoulder, jolting him awake. Startled, he scanned the dark forest, only to notice a tiny, elderly woman standing on the stump, her wrinkled form clad in tattered black garments.

"Hello up there, I'm Schnickelfritz," the wrinkled-skinned lady greeted. "I'm a Flemglobber."

The Dragon, The Prince, and The Flemglobber

"Hello down there, I'm Hipple, a prince," he replied promptly.

Curious, Prince Hipple inquired about Schnickelfritz's presence in Fargessen Forest.

"I live here," she answered. "Fargessen Forest is my home."

Apologizing for his abruptness, Prince Hipple expressed the urgency of his mission.

Schnickelfritz nodded knowingly. "Yes, I'm aware," she said.

Perplexed, the prince questioned how she knew.

"We Flemglobbers have aided your royal family for generations," she explained. "I was assigned to you by the Head Flemglobber, The Duke of Hurl, himself. Consider me your personal Flemglobber, here to assist you, especially now, just before your favorite holiday of Hanukkah."

"That must be why my father, the king, sent me here into Fargessen Forest to find you," remarked the prince. "We have a problem—a big one. My father believed I was old enough to seek your assistance."

"Your father made a wise decision," acknowledged Schnickelfritz. "I've been observing you and the kingdom for some time now. I understand your predicament and am honored to offer my help in person."

Prince Hipple's excitement surged. "Then you can rid us of Finnog the dragon in time for our Hanukkah celebration!"

Schnickelfritz tempered his enthusiasm. "Not so fast," she cautioned. "It's not quite that simple."

Confused, the prince pressed for clarification.

"It's like this," explained Schnickelfritz patiently. "If I were to swiftly resolve this problem for you now, you'd return whenever faced with another challenge, expecting a quick fix. It's not sustainable."

Prince Hipple pondered her words, realizing the importance of a more enduring solution.

"I don't understand," admitted the prince.

"This is a learning lesson," Schnickelfritz clarified. "I'm not here to solve your dragon problem single-handedly."

"Then who will?" inquired the prince anxiously. "If we don't act quickly, Fargessen won't have Hanukkah this year!"

"I'm under strict orders to assist you in solving your problem," Schnickelfritz replied.

"Let's not waste time, then! We need to act fast!" urged the prince.

An Olde Hanukkah Tale

"Patience, young prince. I have an idea," Schnickelfritz interjected. "At this very moment, there are eight brave knights at St. Bernard of Dogma monastery on Mount Batten. They're there to heal using the steam from Bach's Spring. Seek their aid."

Eagerly, Prince Hipple asked for more details.

"Approach Abbot Costello at the monastery and request the assistance of these knights in

dealing with Finnog," Schnickelfritz explained. "With their valor, we may yet solve our dragon problem in time for Hanukkah."

Prince Hipple expressed gratitude to Schnickelfritz before departing Fargessen Forest and making his way to St. Bernard of Dogma monastery atop Mount Batten near Hamilton Beach.

Approaching the monastery, Prince Hipple spotted eight horses in the corral and heard the sounds of squires repairing armor, evidence of the knights' recent battles, mostly against dragons.

Entering the Monastery Grand Hall, he introduced himself to Abbot Costello and greeted the weary knights seated at a wooden table, their exhaustion evident from recent adventures. Despite their fatigue, the knights rose to greet him, introducing themselves and their squires with formal respect.

One by one, each knight shared their reasons for seeking healing at St. Bernard of Dogma monastery.

"I am Sir Vaylence of Subject," began the first knight, accompanied by his squire Vic Tim.

An Olde Hanukkah Tale

"We came seeking relief from my 'private eye' and 'shandel ears'."

Next, Sir Charge of Feez, with squire Cal Cuelatror, revealed his ailments. "I have a 'gold finger' on one hand and 'butter fingers' on my other," he confessed.

Sir Prize of Party, accompanied by squire Eve Vent, then spoke. "I suffer from an 'iced' chest and 'weather veins'," he explained.

Following suit, Sir Ramic of Tyle, with squire Moe Zaic, disclosed his issues. "I have a 'semi colon' and 'knee monia'," he lamented.

Sir Min of Mount, with squire Audie Yunts, revealed his troubles next. "I deal with a 'chris chin' and 'euchar wrist'," he admitted.

Next, Sir Rupp of Maple, accompanied by squire Moe Lasses, shared his struggles. "I need relief from a 'funny bone' and 'bottle neck'," he sighed.

"I am Sir Rappy of Wool," announced the seventh knight, with squire Terry Cloth. "I suffer from 'macaroni elbow' and 'missile toe'."

"I am Su Shi of Rau," declared the eighth

The Dragon, The Prince, and The Flemglobber

knight, accompanied by squire Teri Yaki. As she bowed, her helmet fell off her head, revealing long, straight black hair. "I am the only woman among a lineage of male Samurai warriors. I've come from France after battling dragons to heal 'my rose hips' and a 'French foreign lesion'."

Prince Hipple welcomed the knights, expressing the kingdom's dire need for their aid.

However, Sir Charge of Feez explained their inability to assist immediately due to their ongoing healing process from the steam of Bach's Spring.

Prince Hipple interjected, emphasizing the urgency of their situation.

As the knights questioned the nature of the emergency, Prince Hipple prepared to elucidate.

"Allow me to explain," implored Prince Hipple. "We're facing a colossal problem—a dragon, to be precise. This isn't just any dragon, but a formidable, fire-breathing one."

"So what?" questioned Sir Ramic of Tyle. "We've vanquished countless dragons of all sizes across kingdoms near and far," boasted Sir Min

An Olde Hanukkah Tale

of Mount. "Dragon-slaying is our specialty. Haven't you heard of our exploits in the town criers' announcements or read about them in the newspapers? Our ads and posters are plastered all over the kingdom!"

"But this dragon is different," Prince Hipple insisted.

"What makes this dragon so special?" inquired Sir Rupp of Maple.

"This one is the largest and fiercest we've encountered," replied the prince.

"So?" countered Sir Rappy of Wool. "We've faced many huge, fire-breathing dragons before. Just look at the countless dragons stenciled on our shields—they represent each one we've conquered."

Prince Hipple paused, then inhaled deeply.

"Ever heard of... Finnog?" he asked.

"FINNOG?" exclaimed all eight knights in unison. "OY! V'EY!"

"That huge, fierce, fire-breathing dragon?" questioned Su Shi of Rau.

The Dragon, The Prince, and The Flemglobber

"Yes," confirmed Prince Hipple. "Finnog is currently blocking the main road to Tolemac. It's causing complete gridlock, with Hanukkah just around the corner."

"Hanukkah?" echoed Sir Vaylence of Subject.

"The Festival of Lights?" added Sir Charge of Feez.

"The holiday commemorating the Maccabees' victory?" chimed in Sir Ramic of Tyle.

"The miraculous oil lasting eight days instead of just one day?" queried Sir Prize of Party.

"Yes, THAT holiday," affirmed Prince Hipple. "Imagine a year without Hanukkah: no potato pancakes, no dreidels, no chocolate 'gelt,' and worst of all, no presents!"

The knights huddled together, murmuring quietly among themselves.

"I don't know about you knights," Su Shi of Rau whispered to the others, "but restoring Hanukkah to the Kingdom of Fargessen is a worthy cause, especially at this time of year."

An Olde Hanukkah Tale

"It's our next valiant quest," added Sir Rupp of Maple. "And this time, we can do it right here, in our own kingdom!"

"We'll rest tonight, plan our attack, and breathe in more steam from 'Bach's Spring'," promised Sir Min of Mount to Prince Hipple. "Tomorrow, we'll do our best to rid your kingdom of Finnog in time for Hanukkah."

"Thank you, brave knights," Prince Hipple said gratefully. "You'll be honored guests at our Hanukkah celebration, and forever in our debt."

The prince left the knights to rest and plan at St. Bernard of Dogma monastery, returning to Kenahora Castle to inform his parents of the plan.

At sunrise, the knights set out one by one to confront Finnog, allowing for backup if needed. Throughout the day, each knight attempted to coax Finnog away from the road, growing increasingly tired and battered.

As evening fell, the exhausted knights returned to the monastery, one by one, their efforts evident in their weary appearance.

The Dragon, The Prince, and The Flemglobber

Seated in the monastery's hall, the knights recounted their futile efforts to dislodge Finnog.

Sir Vaylence of Subject, lacking essential gear, found his sword shattered against Finnog's armored hide.

Sir Rupp of Maple's offering of two jugs of syrup backfired when Finnog demanded a breakfast buffet of pancakes and waffles.

An Olde Hanukkah Tale

Sir Prize of Party's noisy horns briefly startled Finnog, who simply used Sir Rupp's jugs as a pair of makeshift earplugs.

Sir Min of Mount's lecture fell on the dragon's deaf ears, Finnog unfazed as he continued devouring lieberries, oblivious to the knight's pleas.

Sir Charge of Feez attempted to scold Finnog for unpaid taxes, only to realize the dragon couldn't hear due to syrup-jug earplugs. Frustrated, he presented Finnog with a stack of tax forms, hoping to teach him a lesson in fiscal responsibility.

Sir Rappy of Wool's plan to annoy Finnog with loud, off-key guitar strumming and singing failed miserably, leaving him with sore fingers and a sore, very hoarse voice.

Sir Ramic of Tyle's effort to startle Finnog with loud ceramic tile banging fell flat as the dragon remained unfazed, preoccupied with his lieberry feast.

Su Shi of Rau recounted her futile attempts at using martial arts moves on Finnog, whose thick skin rendered her efforts ineffective. Exhausted and defeated, all eight knights

The Dragon, The Prince, and The Flemglobber

slumped at the table, their spirits low.

King Dom expressed gratitude for their efforts but lamented the lack of progress. Queen Sighs urged them not to give up, emphasizing the impending arrival of Hanukkah and their desperate need for a solution.

Prince Hipple resolved to seek Schnickelfritz's counsel again. The following day, he returned to Fargessen Forest, finding the Flemglobber standing on the same tree stump.

With a heavy heart, Prince Hipple confessed to Schnickelfritz the Flemglobber that despite the knights' efforts, Finnog remained immovable, and Hanukkah drew nearer, threatening to pass without celebration.

Prince Hipple contemplated the disappointment of growing older and the challenges of life. Schnickelfritz, the Flemglobber, handed him a twig to break, illustrating how a single twig snaps easily. Then, she gave him a bundle of eight twigs, which he struggled and failed to break, showing how unity creates strength.

Abbot Costello appeared, revealing his longstanding friendship with the Flemglobbers

An Olde Hanukkah Tale

and his awareness of Prince Hipple's ongoing dilemma with Finnog. He proposed a plan involving the rested knights and the collective effort of everyone involved.

The following morning, Prince Hipple, along with his family, the knights, the monastery's monks, and the townspeople, gathered to discuss Abbot Costello's plan. They then marched to Tolemac's main square, where Finnog, engrossed in eating lieberries, was startled by their approach.

Finnog rose on his hind legs, exhaling a burst of flames, setting lieberry bushes ablaze, warning the crowd to stay back. Abbot Costello calmly requested to speak with Finnog, who complained of hearing difficulties due to aging. Sir Rupp of Maple jokingly asked for his maple syrup jugs back, which Finnog obligingly returned.

Perplexed by their nonviolent approach, Finnog questioned their intentions, expecting weapons. Prince Hipple reassured him they meant no harm, prompting Finnog to listen attentively. Feeling misunderstood, Finnog expressed his desire for peaceful lieberry feasting, puzzled why others viewed him as a threat.

"You're absolutely right," Prince Hipple agreed. "We don't mind if you enjoy lieberry patches. All we ask is for you to move from this road, especially with Hanukkah approaching."

Finnog nodded, realizing the misunderstanding. "I'm not like other dragons. I'm old, with few teeth left in my mouth and fading fire-breathing skills," he admitted.

The dragon explained his struggles as very young, inexperienced, and even abandoned, due to not meeting strict, ferocious dragon standards. "We were so poor I had to drop out of M. I. T. (Monster Institute of Terror). All I wanted was to live in peace and eat lieberries," he tearfully confessed to the assembled crowd.

King Dom empathized, recognizing the parallels between dragons and humans. "Some are good, some are bad," he concluded.

"Thank you for understanding. Now, if you'll kindly show me to a lieberry patch, I promise not to bother anyone," Finnog said, crossing his heart.

"May I suggest a spot near Fargessen Forest?

An Olde Hanukkah Tale

Lieberry bushes stretch for miles, and you won't block any traffic," Schnickelfritz proposed.

Grateful, Finnog's constant flow of gigantic tears, finally and thankfully quickly doused the burning bushes.

"We might have a tiny problem," Prince Hipple noted.
"What's that?" Finnog inquired.
"Well, what do we do now with this huge pile of gooey red stuff left by all the burning lieberry

bushes?" Queen Sighs gestured to the mess. "No worries," Schnickelfritz reassured.

"Really?" Prince Hipple was skeptical.

"Yes, indeed," the Flemglobber confirmed. "We Flemglobbers have been making lieberry products for ages."

"How so?" King Dom inquired.

"We cook lieberries to make jelly, jam, preserves, and syrup," explained Schnickelfritz. "It's what we do best."

Abbot Costello grinned. "I have an idea."

After Fargessen's grand Hanukkah celebration they began creating Fargessen's new sensation: lieberry jelly, jam, preserves, and syrup.

Everyone joined forces to harvest lieberries near Fargessen Forest, cooking them into jelly, jam, preserves, and syrup. Finnog tended to the fires, while the Flemglobbers shared their recipe for processing the lieberries. Meanwhile, the Benedictine monks created St. Bernard of Dogma Lieberry Benedictine Wine and Brandy from the leftover fruit.

An Olde Hanukkah Tale

The brave knights transitioned to salesmen, promoting Fargessen's products alongside the monks' beverages. Queen Sighs found fame writing catchy jingles for commercials with both her nieces, once again, providing musical accompaniment on their 15-string lutes.

As Finnog aged, the people of Fargessen supported him. He rejuvenated at Bach's Spring, improving his fire-breathing abilities and hearing. He became essential to the survival of the Kingdom of Fargessen for lighting fires year-round and clearing snow off the roads in winter.

With his earnings, Finnog built a retirement home for elderly dragons, aided by Sir Charge of Feez managing his taxes. Finnog's proudest moment? Lighting the shamash candle on Tolemac's menorah each Hanukkah, symbolizing his acceptance by the Kingdom of Fargessen.

The Dragon, The Prince, and The Flemglobber

Fargessen became renowned not only for its lieberry products but also for its friendship with the once-feared dragon, showcasing the power of unity and acceptance.

An Olde Hanukkah Tale

The End-ish

www.ingramcontent.com/pod-product-compliance
Lightning Source LLC
LaVergne TN
LVHW011431080426
835512LV00005B/386